CONTRARY-WISE

Also by Vickie Cimprich

Pretty Mother's Home: A Shakeress Daybook
A Quilted Life (with Hazel Durbin)

CONTRARY-WISE

Vickie Cimprich

Broadstone

Library of Congress Control Number 2018936009

ISBN 978-1-937968-43-4

Design & Composition by Larry W. Moore.

Front cover photograph by the author.
Back cover photograph by Jim Cimprich.
Used by permission.

Broadstone Books
An Imprint of
Broadstone Media LLC
418 Ann Street
Frankfort, KY 40601-1929
BroadstoneBooks.com

In grateful memory of my parents

F. Edward and Betty Neff Hucker,

and my mentor

Sandra Cuni

CONTENTS

I.

II.

III.

And when they told me
"God is dead," I answered "He goes fishing every day
in the Kentucky River. I see Him often."

— Wendell Berry,
"The Contrariness of the Mad Farmer"

... it's as though I were fishing with a line: I write
whatever comes to the end of my pen.

— St. Thérèse of Lisieux

I

Nocturnal

Going to bed at night
in Lee County,

you're never for sure
if the whippoorwill you're hearing
is in your mind

or one ridge over.

On Contrary

Mud complicated the woods-way down.

A big old woodpecker-bird's cackle spread whatever
news it knew up and down Contrary Creek. Three days
earlier, when the door of a freight car at the Heidelberg
station slid open, Edmund and Virgil spied something
different that they didn't know was a scorpion. Any
time the patches of ordinary can tear away, all for the
good or not.

The red sanctuary lantern mostly always burned in the
small church on the creek. What it meant was something
now and then some wondered about, maybe decoration
or that somebody's mostly always to home here, miles
down from the ridgetop where the folks would move
when Highway 399 came along to make a way for cars.

Some time into the singing and Latin rumble-prayers
we reached into our pockets and purses for nickles to
drop into what Willie called the minner basket. The
slidey paths to home hid their paynters and copperheads
inside rockhouses and in the backs of trees.

AMONG SOME MEMORIES
remembering L.W.

The day the piano somehow made its way
up the creekbed up to her house
near Belle Point,

the time she took a stand
on Father Schulte's porch and asked him why
she couldn't go with the bigger girls
who got the bishop's scholarships
to Cardome Academy,

the swelter of the day
three Sisters arrived from Bardstown
to teach the summer Bible school:
Aunt Jule welcomed and invited them
to take off their starched bonnets.

"We always leave them on,"
the head Sister said. "Suit yourself,"
Aunt Jule did not reply.

HELEN KEATING, 1886-1973

Caney Creek school at last! Miss Lloyd came out
to welcome me at Hindman. By the time
the car had pulled as far as the hollow's mouth,
we were Alice and Helen. The children sang
"Once More My Soul" to welcome me, harmonies
a bit askew, but not their bows or buttons.
Truly, to be their principal and teacher
was all I'd dreamed, in Pennsylvania.

After I'd had time to settle in,
Alice brought some blooms, redbud she said,
and a vase to decorate my sideboard
(a travel trunk, with doily, looked quite well).
We chatted. "Pippa Passes" was the piece
of Mr. Browning's she admired the most.
Much she knew by heart. Presently
she looked round, admiring the few bits
of home I'd brought, the photograph: my sister
by my side, our solemn communion. We
were twelve. *You must be twins.* Yes, I was proud
to own. Her eyes stopped at the pillow. Three
beads poked out. She said, *Of course you know
how things stand here. All should go well. Just keep
this quiet now.*

            Two factors were involved
in my discernment to move on: She'd said
I couldn't be myself. Moreover, she'd sold
these people short. Each one I met was dear.

But then *God's in his heaven, all's right with the world,*
chuckled Mr. Browning, Bishop Howard
and I, when the bishop and I first wrote
then met. *Your mountains work will be successful,*
he believed. *It's likely you, Miss Keating,
are the one we have been praying for
on Contrary and in Covington, to lead
our mountains school. Take this three hundred now.
Let me know. I'm sure we can get more.*

GRANDMA AND THE PAYNTER
for Lucy

My brother, me and our grandma used to have to walk
down to Contrary to clean the church. While coming
back up the mountain at the back of our house, grandma
heard the paynters in the trees a-beatin their tails, and
she was scared to death. We was all shakin and walkin
and runnin.

Grandma told us to run on ahead and try to make it to
the house to get away. We wanted to wait for her, but
she said, No, you all go on home as fast as you can, and
I'll let the paynter eat on me. She said we was young
and had our whole life ahead of us, and she was old
and it didn't matter.

So we run on to the house to get the pistol and tried to
get back in time to kill the paynter before it got our
grandma. But by the time my brother got to the field at
the back of the house, she was comin through the fence.

Things We Knew

How Contrary worked cause we was a part of it.
Sometimes people's walk-logs would wash away
and they'd have to cut another tree.

They'd carry 50 pound coffee sacks
full of black and butternut walnuts,
and five gallon lard cans full
of blackberries and huckleberries
up the mountain to sell at Heidelberg.

Groundhogs? You'd boil them
then bake out the grease.

FOR A FRIEND
F2 US Navy WWII
12/29/1921 - 4/4/1991

One of the kids who'd boarded on the creek,
whose eyes would glint each time he'd conjure up
assorted memories for me, such as
Miss Helen Keating, when she'd look as if
she'd seen in him the devil. Many would.

Out west, the Civilian Conservation Corps
saw his heyday. Next he'd find himself
in way over his head like thousands more
mountain boys in Cincinnati. Why
not enlist in some convenient war?

AWOL from The Oklahoma, the worst day,
Pearl Harbor's bombing. He got rounded up:
a Honolulu policeman ordered him
up on a porch, the person's blackout shades
were not drawn. Fell backwards off. Too much
pandemonium to diagnose
or treat a non-combat head injury,
not factored in to any exoneration.

Assigned then to The Louisville, engines
baffling wits he tried to muster up.
Undesirable discharge. Organic
Brain Damage got finally rubber stamped
on files that would belie his best intents.

All told his wife not to marry him.
Then why? "Well, I had this broken ankle
at the time. . . ." Ain't any love just grand?

I loved him differently, indifferent to
his roustabouting stratagems. Sundays
I watched him trouncing up the aisle. Behind
the sanctuary was the kitchen where
no wooden kneeler with its curtained screen
would serve to hide one sinner from the next.

One Laetare Sunday, sick of Lent,
I steered the three of us to Natural Bridge.
The chair lift up, and after that the feast
at the lodge restaurant. (This was the year
the dam at Tellico did not get built.
Fresh from Paul Harvey's take on this he said:
Them fish they're serving? They're snail darters. Yum.)

Towards the end he quit the lithium,
laid rubber through four counties, spending what
should have been house money. Finally
thunked down, the V.A. psych ward, Lexington.

Wrote me: *I'd like to have an Incense Slinger*
like at Benediction, a hum dinger;
the smell of Incense tickles in my spine.
My girlfriend's St. Therese and she's real fine.

Thérèse's deathbed promise: *I will spend*
my heaven showering roses down on earth.
Her petals mixed with the tobacco shreds
he'd hold in fingers Camels-colored brown.

Sister Francis Anne Durbin
(Margie Anne)

Congregation of Divine Providence
Born in Estill County, December 15, 1932

Daddy worked at the oil refinery at Pryse. Uncle Hamilton
got caught in the fire there, one of the men that didn't live.
Our Aunt Rachel used to send us one of those peppermint
bars like this, we took a hammer and cracked it for eating.

We used to go down Contrary Creek, to our summer vacation
school. I was probly seven or eight at first. From Estill, we'd
walk on the railroad, if a train didn't come, up to Old Landing,
but if a train came you had to get off and get on the dirt road.
Then up to the top of the mountain, cross the hill, down to
Contrary Creek to have our catechism. Well actually it sounds
like a long way, but it wasn't to us. And you weren't afraid. In
those days the worst thing you came upon would be a whiskey
still.

Sisters came. Different ones ever summer. They had the
older kids with that catechism . . . I can't remember what the
name was. Oh. Baltimore. Baltimore Catechism. We sang
hymns in English. You had to learn to listen to the Latin words
but I don't think any of us ever learned the Latin. The Sisters
read the Bible to us, the New Testament. Most of the time not
more than twenty children. The older kids could read, and
then they would read it to the next group down. Ever once in
a while some of the older women from Ravenna who were
more educated came to help.

Then we'd get to go outside and play, ring-a-round-the-rosy,
hopscotch. We marked the dirt with sticks. Ever once in a
while we would pick up some boy or girl that weren't Catholic
that wanted to come cause we had fun. Sometimes they used
to make fun of us: "Here comes the Cat-licks!"

Father Oscar Poole was the priest, and so his mother lived
with him. She always had something for us, cakes, cookies,
maybe some homemade candy or somethin. We loved ever
minute of it.

The Sisters were so good. Religious habits? Never bothered me. I wore the CDP habit until we changed ... what? About ten years ago? The Sisters taught us to write letters to other places that was havin the same things and we would get back answers from these. We loved those things. And they would write back. Sometimes because they were from better schools than ours, we'd get little gifts from them. Little cards or little things like you'd get out of cereal boxes.

The Sisters were trying to get us to know who we were, who we worshiped, what happens to us in our life, what happens to us when we die. And the things that we had to know like fasting, all the Lenten days. My father took Lent very, very seriously. And you know what? The children tried to do it too. They wanted to do what Daddy did.

What priest was it when they decided they would move the church? See I entered the convent, the 1956 area, so I'm not sure when a lot of these things happened. My brothers and my cousins worked with the ones that were movin it. They literally carried a lot of it. There's pictures of them movin it, up the church hillside. They did a really good job. But see, when the old homestead burnt down, everything that was in it went with it, and there was nothing left over and my one brother died in the fire.

Our cousin Roy was the one getting that church moved up because it was decaying so bad down in the creek. He's also the one who paid a lot of money to keep it up.

When people used to talk – or even now – about people in the mountains, they have no sense of the people in the mountains' wisdom of what the world is, of all the things they have to take care of in the wilderness, the gardens, the water, they have no idea of how people had to take care of that because they had to live. You know, a city person, there's so many things they don't know about people who live in these woods.

I thought it was so interesting how we get so interested in the background but we're not really interested in the front.

Like a Man

The one who was the bishop at that time
was goin all around, to all these parishes
for Confirmation and to check on things.

There come a really real hard rain
when something was goin on at St. Therese,
and they tried to tell this bishop
that you cain't get across; the creek
just comes up and you cain't drive thu it.

He didn't listen. He's gotta do
what he wants to do. He got down in there
and got stuck in Contrary, and they said
he cussed just like a man.

WE HEARD TELL

One reason the creek got named Contrary
might have been the way Kentucky River
backflowed at its mouth.

▶

One time old Father Poole went walking
back the branch. He sniffed the air
and then got mad.

He wasn't mad there was a still
on church land, wasn't mad a parishioner
made the still, but he was mad
nobody'd offered him a taste.

▶

A couple guys of the visiting team were sitting behind
about 20 nuns who were rooting for the home team.

One guy says, "Well, I think I'll move to Alabama:
they only got about 10% Catholics there."
The other fellow said, "Well, I think I'll move to Mississippi.
They only got 5% Catholics there."

One of the nuns turned around and said, "Why don't you
go to hell? They don't have any there."

A Neighbor

A limb fell on his head once,
knocking him out cold.

He never was the same,
and didn't have too much to say

but it was always pleasant.

Contested

Three tunes were bequeathed

by the whippoorwills that sang
thirty years ago nearby the porch
where Donley and Kate
would pass their days.

The crows demanded
to inherit them, but the barred owl
probated that they never would.

II

DIRECTIONS TO ST. THERESE

Pass 1,257 rampant redbud trees, 17 Baptist churches and
2 yard sales. There be double semis barreling south on I-75.
Near Corinth, one will sideswipe your '87 Chev Celebrity.
Never mind.

Briefly mourn the turkey vulture whose impact pits your
windshield just before Richmond. Then east on 52. At
Ravenna, six of one, half a dozen of the other to go over the
mountain or through the one-car-at-a-time underpass and
follow between Kentucky River and the railroad. Estill County
pasture land allows for cattle and corn fields. Then begins the
climb. Wet black crags overhang the big curve near the right
turn onto KY 399. If you pass the goat farm you've gone too
far.

The gravel drive will sneak up on your left. Put the car in park
at the base of the hill and clamber out to lift the rusty iron hook
from the pine tree, then let down the old cable dangling its
same old red rag.

Before you unload the week's food and six gallons of drinking
water, get the key from Edward to unlock the front door of the
church. As you walk up the threadbare carpet of the aisle,
dodge the first five of many hellbent inmate wasps. It'll be
some double take when you recognize one with her non-
stinging barb as an Ichneumon.

Another key is hidden in the sanctuary I won't say where.
Take the pyx out of your shirtfront pocket and lay it inside the
tabernacle on the linen doily some Sister or the other
embroidered 67 years ago. Dust off the old scrap lumber
seiza bench so you can kneel, welcomed within an inch of
your life.

EARLY APRIL

Wasps quiesce
in an unheated room,
one on the curtain hem
another on the prie dieu's side.

The day's weather folds around the selves
inside our houses and our double-wides
along the Heidelberg Road.

It's othering just now.

AFTER THE THAW

Frog eggs like grapes
cluster on the fallen sticks
in puddles alongside Contrary.

Two Rottweilers on Contrary

Sycamore children along the creek got tall,
their thin trunks sprouted from old cuts or burns.
Small fleshy lichens on the wet, dead trees,
the colors and the shape of turkeys' fans.

Sheltowee Trace Trail led south beyond
what was familiar. Through some briers and weeds
a clapboard house appeared. It had a dank
above-ground pool. Just there came charging out
the vicious dogs. Now what to do? Ahead,
above, the old charred railroad trestle loomed.
No way up or out. Behind a tree
I hid. Should I evade or meet their eyes?

My daypack held the hope. I reached inside.
Out with a blunt Swiss army knife and then
 I dusted off the lint from wedges of
some chunks of Brie. Then we three all made nice.

Said Edward later on: Some man walked there
and met those dogs. He had to shoot one
in the head.

Too bad the man forgot
to pack his cheese.

KENTUCKY COBRA

"Don't take another step,"
warns Hargis near the start
of our spring wildflower hike,
"you won't if you're smart."

It takes me half a mile
down to Contrary's banks, to find
the word hognose to apparate
inside in my creaky mind.

"Next of its ploys," then brags
the docent who is me, "I think,
would have been roll over,
then play dead and stink."

VENERATION

Wood-betony's
maroon blooms bow
in all the directions.

BLOODROOT

One leaf, so wide,
cups its lobes like a hand
around the white bud.

Send down, then,
under the dead leaves,
to where skin scrapes away
around the breadth of the blood root.

There in the mud
are your fingers roots?
How much of your blood
would it take to dye a shirt?

You get off your knees,
you straighten your back.

The message clings in thin crescents,
dirt under your nails,
the small moons
that will wash away.

Pileated

     Poplar

to sycamore

   to walnut

goes the tallest woodpecker

    carried like the prophet Habakkuk

by its blood crested head.

Sassafras

Some leaves
fit the air like a mitten.

Some,
like the hoof print
of merychippus.

Dig some up
or hack it off.
Take it home.

You'll have good tea
and a thumb pad
that stays brown
for a week.

WOOD THRUSH

No day or loneliness
can ever be too long,

no July day too hot
when she is close

and never seen.

MOCKINGBIRD

This mockingbird perched high

in me is teaching back
to the sad quiet birds

all the songs they used to know.

TARPIN

Some same terrapin or other
comes craning her neck at
this white clapboard house.

How long, she wonders,
can such a shell
persist in her way?

Leather legs
sag an hour or so
to give it time to pass.

AUGUST

Rainbow over Belle Point
expires between sunset
and sheet lightening.

The first cool air
in four days bolts east
exploding. Utility wires
droop from the poles
that lean over the road.

Tonight the evening primroses
stay closed.

November

From somewhere out of deep inside
the Warm Morning heating stove
comes the throat-singing
of Tibet's Gelugpa monks.

The risen heat, as fires catch,
will summon Sufi wasps
who dervish in the attic.

Sooted webs, three Advents old,
mark the church door's lintels.

Rotgut, Ruin and Roses

Sun comes out a little, but I shiver.
Snow redeems another day
from the plans I had for it.

Nothing in me wants to burn,
but I'm smoldering on edge,
tied by thought, driven closer
than desire goes.

Paint's flecked off the titular buds
on the Little Flower's statue, donated
In memory of Ignatz Sterusky.

The afternoon pinches my nose
and tries to pour
its stern spoonful of nothing
down my throat.

To take any name is in vain.
All my pride, a compost pile;
my brightest conception,
a sawdust-wood-ash shit box.

On such a day last year
I celebrated my income tax.
Shake up another Pepsi,
explode the silence with gossip.

LIKE THE MONA LISA

Two young girls come visiting
to pass some time with me.
They like to pass prayer notes
inside the tabernacle in between
my visits, when it's empty.

In the rooms behind the church
they stop, amazed,
before the full-face photo
of Thérèse. Says Sarah Hope:
She looks just like the Mona Lisa!

Two young girls come by
to pass some time with me
and in the course of this and that
they meet the way
the saint's eyes see.

Visiting

Drunk as a skunk, he parked his truck
on the other side of the cable, staggered
up the hill into the church, and sagged
onto his knees at the sanctuary
of the church he wouldn't enter sober.

I fed him coffee and scrambled eggs,
played him "Tennessee Waltz" on my recorder,
and drove him home.

When I visited next he was outside
his trailer, burning insulation
off some copper wire.

An Odd Hoc Crisis Action

A few years back it was announced
the 1948 church basement's caving in;
so they'd have to take the building down.

Some days later in a midnight raid,
the men crawled in through a low window,
shoring up the church's one foundation

with railroad timber braces.

THE RUMMAGE
to Gin

Musty rooms,

their wallpaper flowers
with sixty seasons' bragging rights
unmitigated by any central heat,

get heaped floor to ceiling
when the pickup trucks from Michigan pull in.

Old rooms, old churchhouse
riddled with live and dead wasps and prayers.
Rummage Sale each Friday
in the back rooms the priests and nuns
left out of for town in '66.

You wade in, I climb a stack,
duck the ceiling, and
hurl you boxes labeled
APPALACHIAN CLOTHES.
Shoot, customers will be just as pleased
as if they said PIERRE CARDIN.
(What the heck is *Appalachian*, anyhow?)

CHILDRENS FALL or
WOMENS or MENS PANTS
get laid on pineboard trestle tables
with doorknob holes cut in them
before they were unneeded
to keep somebody out or in.

Ceramics and beads, shoes, doilies,
for a quarter a thing – 50 cents for Levi's.
Take home three paper sackfuls for less
than the price of one plastic from Maloney's.

You, Mossie and I plan a weekly quilting.
Plenty fabric, anyway, roomfuls of it
like Rumpelstiltskin's gal had straw.
Aw, we can't sew, we said;

I whined, These blocks don't match,
the patterns and the colors clash.
The more the better, says you.
You were right. The Nine Patch
made us each a marvel to ourselves.

Between Fridays, you saved out
special things for me. Earthshoes
never worn, two years outmoded:
"Why, nobody'd wear um but Vickie."
And I would, glad-stepping spine a-tilt
between Kentucky and California
til half my heels pertner met the ground
right through them.

Sick of clothes, one night
you brought a thermos and two cups.
In a church pew, we drank ginseng tea
and laughed like drunks,
aye, Lordy.

PURIFICATORS

Altar linens most of us forgot
are brown blood stained

from mouse births or hemorrhage
from warfarin. Claw marks

separate some threads
of crooked-y red crosses
someone handstitched once upon a time.

Remnants

Near the concrete pillars
and the rows of mossy stones
down at the old church site,
there's the odd rusted cooking pot,
several japonicas, clumps of daylilies
and the old spring house.

Today, Bud cans, a tire rim
and bare dirt eroding where four wheelers
gouge their ways.

A quarter mile upstream,
a roadside pool's a-stir
with foot-long black salamanders,
yellow spotted, who tend
their cache of pearly eggs.

Patches of 8s

Some days later in the laundry

the mud that'd caked on my jeans cuffs

sluffed off a live red-brown spider,

one who likely had joined my leg

last Tuesday on Swift Creek Camp Trail,

at Red River Gorge. How some things

you don't even know might be there,

or here, can maybe bite. Or not.

French Braiding the Garlic

Strands so far off a straight course
by now confound my plans of
45 years back, gone awry
of any comprehensive grasp.

At Camp Marydale then, counselors
insisted ways for hanging whistle-
authority from the plastic lanyards'
varicolored loops. So I learned,
those years before Marydale got sold,
some few said down the river.

Pods I poked into the dirt last spring
outdo the weeds. Blades dry
to straw. Sort three to a bunch,
twelve to a braid. My beautician mom
knew the trick to borrow
if a clump runs short.

Finished, it can stretch
to the ash-blond color of my hair
before I knew this much.

Elegy for a Suitor

My dear friend,

Thank you for returning my book,
and for the windows in my life
we bashed open with the broomstick

we almost jumped.

Vickie

One Holy Rule of Contrary

Anytime

warm-blooded opportunities
come by, grab hold
like a tick,

but let them pesky impulses
flit on past like gypsy moths.

III

SOJOURN, REDWOODS ABBEY
Whitethorn, California

Between one map and another,
I've lost my co-ordinates, Uncle Louie,
Thomas Merton. Between creeks,
Contrary and Mattole,
I mourn the loss
of the mountains that loved me.
United Air's flight lines
gash that path
like whitethorns my legs.

It is hours or days from where
one light, then another,
goes on in pre-dawn Lee County.
The school bus passes
the white frame house that was my home.
Off Sheltowee Trace Trail by there
and in Sinkyone Wilderness near here,
I look to the people and trees
who are still standing.

The fixed stars, the sun passing over,
pour oil over such distances.

The urge to go or stay
goes or stays.

DISCERNMENT, ON SKIS

O why could not my own druthers
taut as the tow rope I hold behind
all this horsepower bring deliverance?

Lord, bid me come. Draw my skis
skimming over the old roofs, abandoned farms,
bones of squirrels, woodchucks, deer
fathoms below in Buckhorn Lake.

Do not forsake me here
beating my thoughts
like some ghost with a flat broom
and her fraying rug.

PENTECOSTAL

Preacher Turtle Woman let on
it'd be real slow. It is.
Real slow. So
on I wait, back home near Cincinnati,
where the water travels under wheels
below a steel bridge floor.

It's something to do,
wave my hand a little in the air,
burn some fingers, find whatever
five torches can sing to.

What turns up
isn't faithful at the speedway.
Dissolves most before the focused lens.

One way into the Ohio is the Licking.
Plunge your face into its South Fork's shallows
where so many mother mussels nestle.
Take a ride on a dead cow
from the '97 Falmouth flood, or on
one of a hundred thousand plastic jugs
from far as Paintsville. Other-wise:
at Carrollton, Kentucky River gives the all
it got from North and Middle Forks
that joined at Beattyville. Just downstream
of there, Contrary Creek puts in its mite.

These reels of gray circles
in the brown barn dances of streams
lift me like breath; they smash my bones
against the rocks or posts,
when I fall through the net
my prayers have woven.

Shellback's pulpit
sounds the altar call.
Let me tumble through my words
and come out wet.

THE ROAD AND THE TRUTH AND . . .

*to the memory of the 26 miners killed at
Blue Diamond Company's Scotia mine,
March 9, 1976.*

When Governor Bert T. Combs came
to build the Mountain Parkway
some called him messiah
to a godforsaken place.

In Frankfort many scoffed:
"A road to nowhere."

Not so. A road to back to
where that road got started:

as Lawyer Combs
champions Blue Diamond,
Scotia makes
a necessary detour.

LEXINGTON V.A. HOSPITAL

The Old Man's pipe smoke
went stale in these halls.
Wages of war here are paid
in urine specimens, wheelchairs,
janitorial supplies and long waits.

Young orderlies
carry the inalienable secret
from room to room;
young social workers
carry files in their hands.
Oxycontin scripts
sure can earn some ready cash.

Everything good and beautiful in Kentucky
is framed behind plexiglass
on the cafeteria walls.
Outside in the park,
the valor of inchworms
also merits stars.

It Takes a Poplar

Some of us here and now forget
a lot of what we used to know,
wasting little time
undoing work it took a poplar
sixty years to do.

Truckbeds of raw
and canted logs
barrel north and south
between the clear-cut hills.

Can anyone tell anymore
where a good bee tree
can be found?

(The coyotes are back,
and bound to kill our little dogs.)

Locusts

Skin sloughs off my feet bottoms
and the collection of locust shells
on top the old whiskey barrel mounds up.

Evenings I find one,
another hull of a happy bug
who skimmed up, unseen whirred,
high up in the greeny heat.

One hide I found bellies up,
death grip on a coleus stem.
That's style. Like a pharaoh
or a Roman pope, staged under
a canopy, mauve and wing-green waving,
above your most solemn motion.

I put the shells in military formation,
an aeronautical museum, Curtis-Wrights,
outmoded as Eddie Rickenbacker's hat flaps.

I touch noses each to each
in a chitin kiss of peace.
I pet shells. I poke my thumbpad
on sticky nippers. I wedge a fingernail
in the crack. I could never get out
of anything that small.

They grew big flight out of a grub,
they sold their whole life's case
for a pearl of a sample,

these dolls I play with,
waiting for the rest of this me
to turn hard.

ORDINATION ANNIVERSARY
for Jay

The gold is in the crowns
of October's Tulip Poplars.

Frankincense, earth-breath
rising from rock houses in the Gorge
that shelter White Haired Goldenrod.

And myrrh: your winter toast
to the true shapes of hills – bared.

Epiphanies shatter like the piñatas
your blessings broke open
strewing forty years of gifts
over everybody's floors.

November Tallies

The straw and dead root hair gave up the zinnia ghosts'
grip on the dirt so easily after that frost. Manila tombs
labeled with our late professional addresses could hold
whatsoever colored promises, each a shredded skin
nimbus, a dead head. What came home finally to me
that night by the dregs of a votive candle's light would
have to be exhumed by tools now stored away in cellar
cobwebs behind the bicycles, lawn chairs, iron rakes and
grass whip.

So the next morning it all drove me to the monastery
where I helped the nuns pealing and coring Arkansas
Black apples for the seasonal pies, where I could join
them cutting and gouging out the few bad places, talking
of our lives and friends who since the last election had
been threatened or excluded from the local Dollar Stores.

Sooner Dog

You get old.

Carillons of thought, recast
 into one bourdon bell's thick walls,

make a tone so deep
that only the dog in your soul
can hear it

and know when to come.

WEATHER REPORT

By bedtime the storm left us no lights
but old candles in shot glasses.

The ridges again shown dark
out the bedroom windows,
acquitted pro tem
of Kentucky Power's watts
hanging in the branches
like a fancy girl's shimmy.

The children of wolves
never born in Kentucky
on account of D. Boone and his tribes
came panting up our holler
through the wuthering trees.

So we settled in and
took hold again of our selves
as if they were pelts.

OLD LANDINGS

Wheels, feet, claws, roots,
in iron rims, skins, pelts, scales and bark
with horns and wings

by their billions nose around
through the clouds and land,
latching on inside watershed pouches

of the marsupial mountains.

Born Out Back

Moving the three kits took up much of the vixen's
morning. One by one each dangled from her mouth
on their way to the gully that would be their second
nursery. Soon the four were testing the shadows and
rocks and one another above the brush pile den. The
neighbors' riding lawnmower didn't displace them but
a cloudburst did.

Next month the does will air their fawns in this flat
grassy patch. I'll hear creaks of their jaws, chomps of
once or twice chewed grass, moos each makes as her
udder gets nosed and butted.

So morning by morning I drink coffee and pray Lauds
outside. Godmother of the clawed and hoofed, I claim
all arrivals. The creatures by now regard me as an odd
clump of scarce threat; all find my barrenness somehow
moving.

APERTURE

Didn't you ever
take two index cards,
poke a pinhole in one
and hunch over the paper scraps
with the heat on your back

to see in a tiny safe shadow
the sharp silhouette
of a sun eclipse?

This morning's goldfinch
makes its kind of opening
in the way

winter made me blind.

Aubade

A pot of light
is slow cooking on the sky.

Clouds and dark chunks
drift to the edges.

Trees hold out their plates,
tables of faces are spread,
rail cars trickle butter
over a gray wafer.

Nothing has changed,
everything has been changed.

Let the stove coals burn out.

ACKNOWLEDGMENTS

The Lee County Catholic community past and present, its people, pastors, and staff, particularly Frs. Jay Von Handorf and Terry Hoppenjans, and Sister Alice Retzner, O.S.F., who allowed me to stay at St. Therese for many years' residence and private retreats.

Rev. Henry B. Schulte, "The Story of the Oldest Catholic Family in the Diocese of Covington," *The Messenger*, Diocese of Covington, August 19, 1927.

Paul A. Tenkotte, "Settlement Schools, Catholic," in *The Encyclopedia of Appalachia* (Knoxville: University of Tennessee Press, 2007).

Dappled Things, "On Contrary," "November Tallies"; *Coffee & Chicory*, "Bloodroot"; *Journal of Kentucky Studies*, "Helen Keating"; *Mountain Life and Work*, "The Road and the Truth and . . ."; *Pine Mountain Sand and Gravel*, "Elegy for a Suitor"; *Plainsongs*, "Aubade" (as "Alba"); *Poetry as Prayer: Appalachian Women Speak* (Wind Publications, 2004), "Locusts"; *The Single Hound*, "Pentecostal"; *Still: The Journal*, "Nocturnal" (as "Compline").

Cover photo, "Michelle in Contrary Creek," Vickie Cimprich. Back cover author photo, Jim Cimprich.

About the Author

Northern Kentuckian Vickie Cimprich writes of many good and/or interesting times in the Eastern Kentucky mountains.

Her poetry collection *Pretty Mother's Home – A Shakeress Daybook* (Broadstone Books, 2007) was researched at the Shaker Village of Pleasant Hill, Kentucky with support from the Kentucky Foundation for Women. The Foundation's mission is to support feminist artists engaged in social change. With the Shaker poems, as well as her article "Free and Freed Believers and Affiliates of African Descent at Pleasant Hill, Kentucky," in *The Register of the Kentucky Historical Society*, Vol. 111, No. 4, Autumn 2013, she shares enlivening awareness of the Shakers' egalitarian convictions and practices.

Other KFW grants assisted in her participation in the 1999 Spoleto Symposium per Scrittori, as well as visits to French Cistercian abbeys where a 12th century tradition of land-holding and stewardship practices continues.

Her work has appeared in *A Quilted Life*, with Hazel Durbin (Contrary Bear Track Press, 2002), *The African American Review, Bigger Than They Appear: Anthology of Very Short Poems* (Accents Press, 2011), *Dappled Things, Inscape, The Journal of the Association of Franciscan Colleges and Universities, The Journal of Kentucky Studies, The Licking River Review, Mediphors, The Merton Journal, The Mom Egg, Pine Mountain Sand and Gravel, Plainsongs, Poetry As Prayer: Appalachian Women Speak* (Wind Publications, 2004), *Seminary Ridge Review, The Single Hound, Still - the Journal*, and "Waypoints." She has taught English at Lees College, Northern Kentucky University, and the University of Cincinnati.